Broken Mirror

By Mr. No One

&

Lucky Smith

Readers Note

This manuscript is a collection of poetry from Mr. No One and Lucky Smith. The premise of this book is a collection of poetry pondering the eternal question to love or not to love. Introducing up and coming poet from Northeast Los Angeles, Mr. No One. Mr. No One being of a Latin descent. He was born and raised in Northeast Los Angeles, California during the front lines of the Chicano community and gentrification. Witnessing the growth and decline of the Los Angeles community. Mr. No One develops his poetry from the standpoint of empath. Mr. No One has been writing poetry since the 1980's to current, inspired by his surroundings and life experiences.

Lucky Smith grew up in the San Gabriel Valley. When she is not eating tacos, she is jumping off cliffs looking for a new adventure. Lucky Smith is a lover of life, constantly growing and evolving to her best self.

The Table of Contents

WHEN

What are your intentions with me?

When will I get hurt again?

How long this time?

Will it be weeks ahead

Months or years

Maybe a lifetime

Will it be pain or anguish

Am I repeating my toxic cycle?

With a new name

A new face

A new body to replace

A new time for me to hurt again

When

By: Lucky Smith

WICKED EARTH

Evil whispers across the land

all the children take my hand.

the dead man stalks he's here to stay.

reminding you'll die someday.

life is haunted dreams

are cursed to live your death upon this wicked earth

by Mr. No One

AGAIN

We ended before we began

To destruction I ran

Knowing this will not end well

I did not want to change you

I was just hoping

You would love me

Now I know

Never to run to you

Again

By Lucky Smith

WHAT SHOULD I DO?

"What should I do"

lost inside looking around

trying to find but nobody found

walking and talking.

questions are asked.

plans for the future

thoughts of the past.

today is the day.

that moment is here

do I say how I feel?

or do stay in my fear.

wanting waiting what should I do?

sitting here with all thoughts on you...

BY: Mr. No One

ONE DAY

He’s patience

Waiting for me to be ready

His limited time

Freely given to me

Texting back within seconds

Promoting me

Believing in me,

when my confidence is shaking

His intentions, he’s made it clear

One day I will be

By: Lucky Smith

WICKED SINFUL

If you are the sin.

I'll be the sinner.

Seduction and lust would be just the beginning.

I'd go to hell and embrace all the flames.

Just for one chance to hear you scream my name.

Your beauty. Your style. Your wicked sinful smile.

The smooth way you dance with desire and romance.

I want you. I crave you.

To taste you within.

Yes! I am the sinner, and you are my sin.

One moment of want.

A lifetime of pleasure.

To feed on your soul.

To covet your treasure.

To hell I would go.

To the Devils domain

To have you just once.

Would drive me insane.

To go crazy forever.

Just to have you for now.

Would be a lifetime of pleasure.

In the dark depths of hell.

An immaculate moment.

Filled with burning desire.

Douse me in flames.

Never put out the fire.

Yes, I am the sinner, and you are my sin.

No more to say.

Except let's begin.

By Mr. No One

SO AGAIN, I TRY

Denying romantic love into my life

Is denying so much

I refuse to deny myself that glimpse of

Food for my soul

While there is no guarantee

how long,

Or who leaves who

Because every relationship will end

In life or death all relationships end

But living in fear to avoid pain

I just can't do it anymore

No matter how many of my tears drench my floor

Growth thrives from love, and pain

So again, I try

And maybe again I will cry.

By: Lucky Smith

"NOW"

Tears that never fall.

Screams left unheard.

broken promises

dreams shattered

lessons that I've learned.

wishing, wanting more.

yet no one to hear my cry's empty words are spoken.

Left behind with harmful lies.

To give and give

and never receive is a concept known to well.

I've tried I've cried I've been denied.

Now left alone inside my shell.

Once was kind and tender.

Now no more do I feel.

They said one day I'd love again.

But my heart I won't let heal.

Never again will i let anyone in.

No more pain for me. For once I was so different.

Now this is who I'm meant to be.

By My No One

ARE YOU HAPPY?

How does it feel
To depend on no one,
Having sex only for fun
No bond
No real connection
No roots planted anywhere
But you are everywhere
How does it feel
To give up on love
To surrender to isolation
Vacating complications
Running from desperation
Do you get lonely
Night after night
Nameless bodies
A different bar,
Another club
So many apps
So many chats
Are you happy?
Or are you lonely

By: Lucky Smith

ERICA

I cherish your joy

The love that you seek

Never give in to the pain that you speak

Hold on to the want the desire to feel.

I pray one day you'll find it and it comes out to be real

I hide from the suffering

I hide from the pain

At times yes, I want it

but it drives me insane

Will one day I find it?

No can tell.

Till that day that it finds me.

I lay in my hell Is it good for my soul? Is it good for my heart?
I don't have that answer.

For its left me apart

I rant and I rage

I'm trapped in my cage

Maybe one day

I'll be free

But for now I'll remain

BY Mr. No One

APART OF ME

Apart of me hope against reality,

Sanity turned into insanity

Maybe I don't love you

You are being a place holder

For my present and past

Gas lighting myself

Into romantic bullshit

A childish daydream

Apart of me wished

Other options weren't so tempting

Maybe we were never friends

We were two strangers fucking

Exchanging bodily fluids

Filling voids in our lives

Love or not, this pain runs deep

Cracking open doors, I sealed

Long ago

Apart me of hope

By: Lucky Smith

SAY NO ONE

How do I share.

Why should I care.

Finding true love Is no longer rare

It doesn't exist.

That happiness is lost in this endless abyss.

My heart is now black

My thoughts are all cold

Yes, I feel lonely as I sit on my own.

No more caresses

No more let's talk.

No more I love you

No more romantic walks.

I've lost all the urge to feel any more

My lust for that life is now What I ignore.

Will I ever again

I'd rather say no

I'll live this life empty

And not hurt any more

By: Mr. No One

THE AFTERMATH OF YOU

Staring up at the white ceiling,

All I'm feeling,

The aftermath of you,

Staring at the blank pages of my dairy,

It's beyond being lonely,

You promised me,

I'm so sorry,

Another birthday

without you,

I'm just staring into yesterday,

All I'm Feeling,

The aftermath of you,

Strangers to my heart,

Lovers in the dark,

My life became your screenplay,

I never wanted it this way,

Nothing satisfies,

The aftermath of you.

By: Lucky Smith

For James C. Roberts

Rest in peace my love.

EMPTY SPACE

Lost to the loss of your warm embrace.

This blackened heart can find no one to replace.

My lonely sleep without you near

No comfort from loss

Only my tears.

Since last we kissed

Since last I lived.

Now only to feel you.

When looking from up above.

An empty bed I dance alone.

An empty house which no longer feels like home

I miss you close

You're now so far.

Oh how wish I could wish upon a star.

To have you again

To hold you tight.

But it's just me here.

In these lonely nights

BY Mr. No One

BURDEN ME

Burden me with honesty, Burden me, Burden me truthfully, Dear god burden me, Burden me with your hostility, don't insult me with falsehood flattery, Or assume that vanity consumes me, Instead burden me, Impress me with honesty, Bravery to vulnerability without guarantee,

Yet the real burden is fear, Fear of stagnation, rejection, affliction, infliction, change. Burdening people with invisible prisons trap within our own minds, nevertheless, burden me freely with love, or better yet let me burden myself to love you. Yes, to love without love being return. Burden me.

Somehow chasing becomes more attractive than living. A daydream lost in translation. The disappearing rainbow, with its fading pot of gold. The next one will be better, the next one will be hotter. Just an excuse to our own self abuse. Just an excuse for us to use. So, I scream burden me with pain. Let me cry, feel, fail and succeed, as I proceeded. Burden me.

By: Lucky Smith

UNBALANCED

Since last you saw me.

Since last we kissed

I've lost the desire to find my bliss.

No more tears from saying goodbye.

I no longer feel I no longer cry.

I'm here alone and it's ok.

In my heartache

From here on I stay

You're now a memory of what use to be.

That love

I once felt.

I will no longer let be.

Goodnight

Goodbye

To all the pain

Hello to my darkness.

Where I'll remain

BY: Mr. No One

YOUR REALITY

I can be your best friend and stay till the end. I can be your worst enemy, and it's whatever you want me to be. You can hate me or love me. Blame me for all your insecurities. Jump from one distraction to another. Still, you won't know who you are. Let your friends and family direct your every move, How does it feel to be a zombie? You'll never be happy, trying so hard to be free, while you're holding on to your leash. Get in your car, and runaway. But how do you escape your own skin? Who's going to win the war raging in your head? You can have an orgy, and still be empty. I can be your lover and forget you when it's over. It's your reality.

Romance sparked from pity. We are so empty. It felt human to care again, the serotonin drowning my brain. Following the aftermath of Oxytocin, whenever I held you. Honesty invited intimacy. As my emotions became reality. I saw your reality. I was only a void filler. It started with pity, fuel by empathy, and ended by apathy. It's your reality.

By: Lucky Smith

END THAT

was it me?

was it you?

was it all the things we use to do?

was I wrong?

were you right?

is it because of how we use to fight?

did we not make up enough?

did we not have reason?

did we not have lust?

was it the times that I'd say no?

was it the lack of trust?

whatever it was.

I no longer need to know...

my past is not my present.

tomorrow is not today.

if I keep holding on so tight.

I'll never get away.

I'm killing what's been left inside.

the thoughts of what should be.

I'm going to squeeze the trigger.

and end that misery.

once I wanted what we had.

now I truly know.

all of it was never real.

and I've got to let you go.

By Mr. NoOne

I'M NOT ASHAMED

I'm not ashamed that
I got a little too weak
At the end my face leak
I'm not ashamed that
I needed you
In the end I was fooled
I'm not ashamed that
I shared a part of me
What I thought was bury
I'm not ashamed that
You fit perfectly
Whenever you were next to me
I'm not ashamed that
I painted you a picture
Of the beast you capture
I'm not ashamed that
I gave you all of me
To you it was nothing
I'm not ashamed that
Another sleepiness night
Lying next to you felt right
I'm not ashamed that
I love you
When it's unreturned
I loved you

By: Lucky Smith

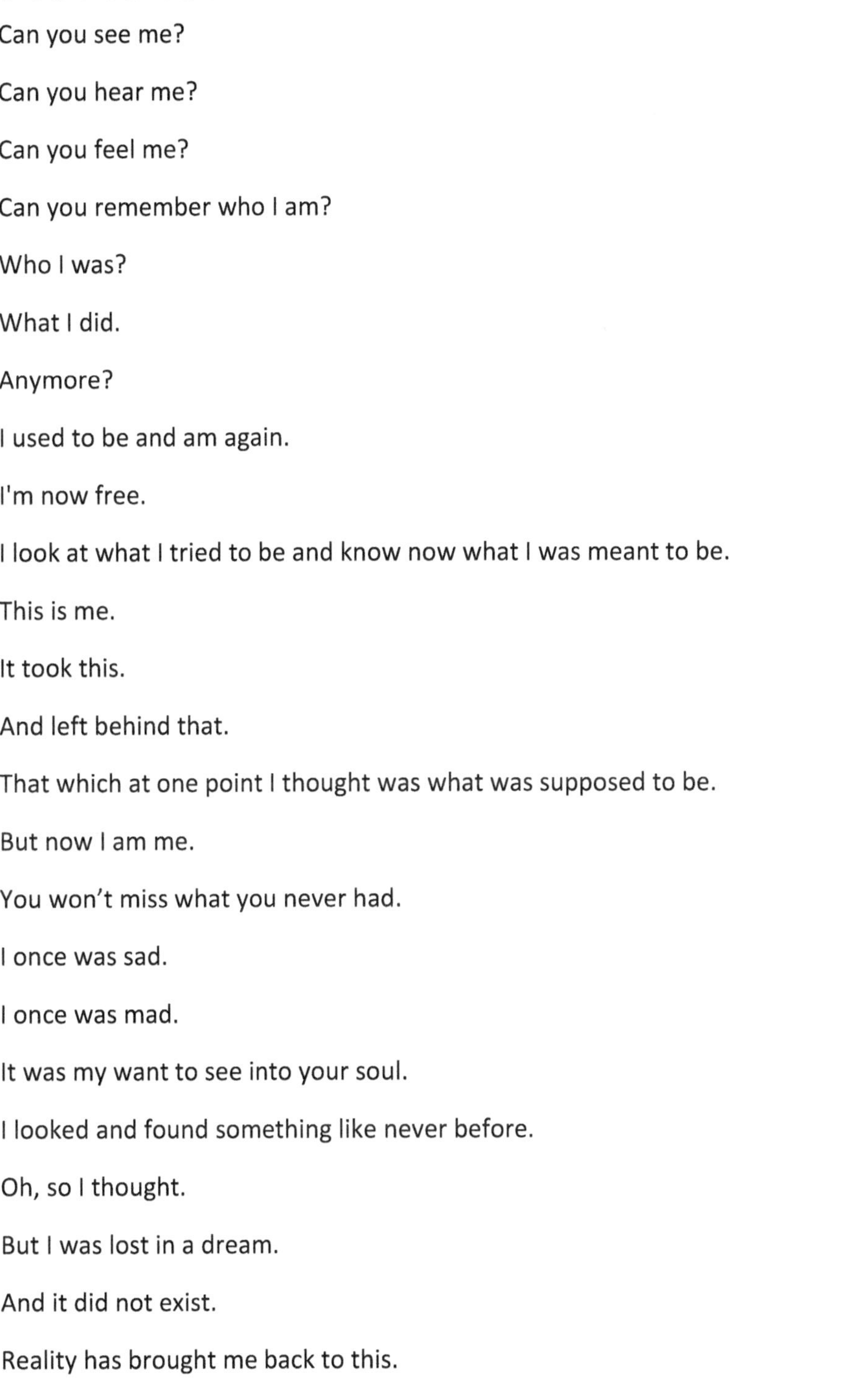

FISNDISHLY FREE

Can you see me?

Can you hear me?

Can you feel me?

Can you remember who I am?

Who I was?

What I did.

Anymore?

I used to be and am again.

I'm now free.

I look at what I tried to be and know now what I was meant to be.

This is me.

It took this.

And left behind that.

That which at one point I thought was what was supposed to be.

But now I am me.

You won't miss what you never had.

I once was sad.

I once was mad.

It was my want to see into your soul.

I looked and found something like never before.

Oh, so I thought.

But I was lost in a dream.

And it did not exist.

Reality has brought me back to this.

This is where I am meant to be I will not resist.

Not behind a white picket fence.

That's not what was meant to be.

I am what I see.

Tormented and made to destroy.

No goodness since I was a boy.

No happy ending.

No kindness.

No more.

This is the playroom.

That I no longer ignore.

By Mr. No One

IMAGAINATION UNDERGONE CASTRATION

Starring at blank screen,
Starving for inspiration,
I can't think,
I drink,
My imagination has undergone castration,
When my safety depends on who is at the station,
I slam my head against the wall,
Independence ripped from me in my fall,
Banging my head against reality,
Surviving and I'm not thriving,
Bouncing in my head,
My enemy has become my bed,
No matter what I can't sleep,
The ghost chasing,
My souls' shaking,
Smiles comes in falsehoods of alcoholic happiness
Falsehoods that are shockwaves of another mess,
It's more than the fact that I'll never be the same,
Or looking for blame,
It's the fact that I no longer hope,
I'm the zombie without the dope,
I hate that I have no control,
Nothing can fill the hole,
It's my life, and it's stolen from me,
This is fucking reality.
By: Lucky Smith

WON'T MEND

Can't unstop this break.

Just don't know how much more of this I can take.

Left alone in a shallow hole.

With no emotional contact to make.

I'm afraid to fall asleep.

When I'm awake I feel defeat.

When I try I'm disappointed?

And my life feels so unworthy.

I've now lost my want to be.

I've decided I can't be me.

I hid away from once being kind and turned into a heartless swine.

And here I am once again.

Being pushed into no end.

Never more

Will I pretend.

I've seen my broken parts wont mend.

By Mr. No One

HE'S NEVER GOING TO LOVE YOU

He's never going to love you,

She nods... she knows it's true,

Yesterday went according to plan,

He's just another foolish man,

They tell her,

Don't be absurd,

He's never going to love you,

She nods...she knows it's true,

She completes her education,

Invest in her dedication,

He'll waste away at some random bar,

He'll never get far,

She'll move on travel the world,

They scream at her,

Don't be absurd,

He's never going to love you,

She nods...she knows it's true,

One day, she'll have another little girl,

She'll get marry,

Teach, write millions of books... she's free,

He'll continue to daydream of the past,

As he longs for anyone... slipping on his flask,

He's trapped inside his fears,

Drowning in his tears,

She'll living in reality,

Without him she's happy,

They whisper to her,

Don't be absurd,

He's never to love you,

She nods...she knows it's true,

He's just another bar fly,

The best thing he did was say goodbye,

His life filled with cheap, stupid women,

His wallet is his only weapon,

They tell her,

Don't be absurd,

He's never going to love you,

She nods...she knows it's true.

By Lucky Smith

CALLING ME

I see darkness

I see hate.

I see violent people fornicate

I smell horror

I smell fear.

Know that the end is drawing near.

I hear whispers in the night.

Voices saying not to fight...

Calling me

Calling me

From the light.

Do what's wrong

Since I cant trust what's right.

Calling me calling me

On the dark.

Blackening my once pure heart.

Can you hear them calling out?

Do they whisper or do they shout?

Be the best at being bad.

Or suffer slowly

Being sad?

Embrace the dark I hold within.

I hear the voices calling me to sin.

By Mr. No One

TIMING SUCKS

Timing failing us now,

Right now...fucking wow,

Trying not to cross

Forgetting who’s the boss

the threshold of friendship,

Saving us another bad trip,

You cast yourself to another rip tide,

More issues than

The stars in the cosmos

I won't deny,

I am running to another wreck,

Empty sex,

Our dreams are coming true,

I am going to miss you,

Who am I going to call?

Or catch me when I fall?

Who will I run to when I can't sleep?

My emotional mishaps are never cheap,

Maybe timing sucks for us,

you I deeply trust,

You see me

for me it's not lust

I am crushing on you,

Nothing I can do,

Timing Sucks

By Lucky Smith

FALSE ROMANCE

what did I miss?

I held on for those moments of eternal bliss.

Never did it happen.

Never did it show.

Happiness is something

I don't think I'll ever know.

why? why not? when? and with who?

not gonna fall for it again.

not something I'm willing to do.

Meet someone. see what is good then all of a sudden.

good turns to hood trying to control me.

restrictions all around I won't be that puppet.

I won't be that clown.

take your beautiful smile

take the words you say

take the look that mesmerizes.

take it all away

not falling for a false romance. N

o not this time.

I've played your game before this time the game is mine...

By Mr No One

NOW I'M READY

I thought I knew what love was, but I don't. You have been all I ever needed all along. You have been there for me every step of the way. As I have in the past filled my body with toxins. You cried for me. I called you dumb, fat, ugly, weak and worthless. Filled you with the shame, I was taught. I chased ideals of perfection, you waited for me. As an adult, I tried to fulfill childhood fairy tales. Regardless, of the reality you hope for me. Never mind the countless times I have tried to delete you from my life. I have ignored you, blocked you and stuff your love far away from me, as I search to fill the black hole inside of me. When you asked for love, I gave you sex. When you needed my emotional investment, I ran away. When you needed my validation, I delivered rejection. You watched as I numb my trauma with numerous of creative addictions. Some of them recycle successful outcomes, and some caused me more turmoil. I guess, I'm here listening, talking and facing you because now I see you love me. It took a narcissistic soul eating dragon, who sucked out my sanity to realize all I needed was you. As I lied strap to a bed, in an insane asylum begging for a cure, you stood by my side. When I had money to burn, you were there. When I had nothing, you were again still there. As I climb mountains searching for a purpose for my life, you trudge along following my every move. I laughed at your feelings, mocked your vulnerability, and belittled your needs. Selfishly, I became the monster I have grown to hate. I screamed at you for feeling, needing and wanting. It took my rock-bottom, to start to appreciate you. I thought I knew what love was, but I don't. I fooled myself into my own image of a relationship guru. I'm sorry for all my cruelty. You are enough, worthy of love, beautiful, smart, and strong. You are perfectly, balanced and flawed. Honesty, as I'm getting to know you, now I'm starting to love you for everything that you are as you are now. Now I'm ready to fall in-love with you. When I say you, I mean myself? I'm finally ready to fall in-love with me.

By: Lucky Smith

CHANCES

A chance to love.

A chance to feel.

A chance to trust.

A chance to forgive.

A chance to prove your worth.

A chance to prove your word.

A chance to succeed.

A chance to make happy.

A chance to be happy.

A chance.

Sometimes all we need is that chance to be our best.

Given the chance you would want given to you or to those you love.

Without that chance you could lose the opportunity.

By: Mr. No One

THROW IT AT ME

I take responsibility for the repercussions of your attempt at a emotional concussion. I was in-love, but it wasn't you. You are a piece of shit but for minute I felt good to love again. while you are judging me, trying to sabotage me. I laugh. fuck you for getting friendship, business, hormones, and life twisted. I am glad I walked away from you. codependency is a bitch. your insecurities it's not on me. but your contempt, hate and self-pity, go ahead blame me. Go and dig deep. Look for my flaws because while your one finger is pointing at me, you forget the four fingers that is pointing back at you. We had good times but none of it justifies any of your lies. My affections are like a light switch. you run away from life that's all on you. go ahead and try to stab me in the back, I see the knife coming and those wounds heal. money, people, sex, status none of it defines me. I have had more then you will ever know. just google me fool. you can't take away from me cause who I am is from on inside of me. Go feel sorry for yourself and cry yourself another track. I still am smiling. your mad cause you burn yourself. I flip everything I encounter. Your just another lesson. Throw it at me.

By: Lucky Smith

BEEN CAUGHT KISSING

I heard it from somebody.

That knows you very well.

They said that you'd been with someone.

And they were sorry to have to tell.

They said you had been talking for some time and that they knew.

That you didn’t care no more about the way I felt for you.

Now I'm not one for rumors.

Or for stories being told.

But I heard it from somebody.

That for a long time you have known.

Now I'm not one for rumors.

I wouldn't normally have concern.

But from the way that you've been lately.

I feel I should listen to their words.

I heard it from somebody.

That you’re kissing someone new.

You’re no longer just talking.

You've now got more things that you do.

They told me that you shared with them that you no longer care.

That I'm just another person.

From a short time, love affair.

Now I'm not one for rumors.

I don’t listen to stories told.

But I heard it from somebody that for a long time you have known.

I’m Not one for rumors.

I wouldn't normally have concern.

But with the way you have been lately

I'd have to listen to their words.

I heard it from somebody that you thought I did you wrong.

You thought that I was with someone, and you used that to move on.

That someone boldly told me that they don’t believe it’s true.

But I heard it from somebody that for a long time has known you...

By Mr. No One

THERE ARE PLACES IN AMERICA

There are places in America

Places I will never want to go

Places I never want to know

Not because of money

Not lack of curiosity

When I was a child

Wanting to visit all 52 states, mile by mile

Now there are places in America

Places I will never want to go

Places I never want to know

Not because of travel restrictions

Not because of pending convictions

Education and being woke,

provokes

A rage inside of me

A destination for equality

Longing to be free

There are places in America

Places I will never want to go

Places I never want to know,

Places where the confederate flag flies

Places where tears can't cry

Places where ghost don't die

An America that's not for me.

By Lucky Smith

(THE TRUTH)
THAT I LOVE YOU

That I love you

is the only truth

That I can't hide from myself.

And it hurts me

deep inside

that you're out with someone else.

But I can't keep chasing after you when it's not me that you want.

But I love you so I'm letting go.

And I hope you're doing well.

It's not easy

Tried to please you.

Tried to show you this is real.

But you left me.

On the sidewalk.

Now I know the end is here.

That I love you.

Is the only truth.

Since all the rest was just a dream.

How can I stop.

Thinking of you now that you don't think of me.

That I love you.

Is the only truth.

That I can't hide from myself.

And it hurts me

deep inside

that you're out with someone else.

And I know now to let you go.

Now that you're with someone else.

By Mr. No One

CONNECTION TO IMMORTALITY

It's been over 10 years since you kissed my lips. Over 10 years since you saved me from me. Still the love that birth between us is still thriving. You in every thought driving. Surviving the ashes of yesterday is the hope that I will see you again. That's the factor for evolution is a safe place for reproduction. You my harbor, as I fought against the rocky ocean storms. I looked for you, my lighthouse. You hand down a seed, into my tainted soil. we watered it, feed it, fertilized it, shelter it, bathed it in the sun, and harvest it. Love takes time to grow, to manifest. Now I get it. Love isn't given, nor taken. It is life that can live or die. Love is shared between lives. The seed starts in its alpha and omega. Then we like any other molecules connects bumps into others' lives. Love multiples, mutates, and more seeds drop. Others grow their own story. Maybe for some like our love, connection to immortality.

By Lucky Smith

APHRODITE

Took a chance.

Wasn't looking but I found romance.

Not the kind where you make puppy eyes.

Not the kind that's based on childish lies.

Not a one-night stand.

Or so I thought.

It seems you just never know.

I found someone that's so much more.

It's not all like the fairytale stories young girls love to hear.

We often tend to disagree and still it all seems clear.

I took a chance

And here I stand.

Though you're not by my side.

Your somewhere thinking of me

With that smile that's ten miles wide.

Don't worry.

I'm thinking about the way you laugh

The way you frown.

Even the way you comb your hair.

It all seems very relevant to me.

Which to others may seem rare.

took a chance.

A chance on love.

I took a chance on you and i.

Though we are not perfect.

Though we don’t agree.

Though we make mistakes.

I think of only you.

I can only hope your thinking of only me.

Because we took a chance.

And found Romance

A love I can’t denied.

By Mr. No One

EVERYTHING I AM

I am drunk,
But this isn't all of me,
I drink because,
I hate reality,
Jack with coke,
Mix it with a little dope,
Another line just to cope,
None of it means anything to me,
The crushing truth I will never,
Be happy,
It's my best,
Disappearing from every test,
I'll never be happy,
This isn't all of me,
Give me space to,
Relocate,
Random bars for futile debates,
Breaking more boundaries and gates,
Location,
Dissertation,
Demons never leave,
It is only hibernation,
Every mistake I made,
Every word I ever said,
Every failure,
My deepest misery,
My favorite written story,
Owner of obfuscation,
Just another citation,
Snap and leave me,
I am drunk,
Maybe this is everything I am.

By: Lucky Smith

UNKNOWN TIMES

I'm losing my memories.

Losing my memories of you.

I'm losing my memories.

I'm losing the memories of what we use to do.

Losing my memories.

Losing my memories of you.

Losing the memory of your smile.

It's not what I'm used to.

It's been a long while now.

We've been apart so long.

It's not what it used to be.

And it seems it's all gone.

I've started to lose my way.

Soon it will just be a dream.

I'm losing the memories of what use to be you and me.

I'm losing my memories.

Losing my memories of you.

I'm losing my memories.

I'm losing the memories of what we use to do.

Losing my memories.

Losing my memories of you.

Losing the memory of your smile.

It's not what I'm used to.

I held on as long as I believed.

That we would be together once again.

I kept thinking we'd find our way.

And be happy in the end.

It's now been a while.

And still we've not found our way.

And now that the memories gone.

It's become too late.

I'm losing my memories.

Losing my memories of you.

I’m losing my memories.

I’m losing the memories of what we use to do.

Losing my memories.

Losing my memories of you.

Losing the memory of your smile.

It's not what I'm used to.

I can’t even remember.

When’s the last time I felt your touch.

I don’t even know.

If you even thought of me as much.

The scent of your skin.

The way that your lips touched mine.

It's all disappeared.

The memory has dissolved in time.

I've lost it all.

I've lost my memories of you.

I've lost it all.

I’ve lost my memories of you.

By Mr. No One

LESSON COMPLETE

You're pushing

But I'm not falling

Cause I'm already down

You're pounding

But I'm not breaking

Cause I'm already broken

Go ahead and take my seed of trust as a token

As you're lying

I'm not believing

I'm running,

You're just as twisted

Messed up and lost as I,

While we both got baggage

There is a problem with your invisible luggage

you will never know where to unpack

The weight keeping you off track

Another fellow addict to the idea of love

Drowning in lies and lust

There was a time

That you were my rhythm and rhyme

I chose you to hurt me

To test me

As I fail miserably

So, I take the answer key

Studying it again

Seeing the pathogen of deceit.

Now this final lesson is complete.

By: Lucky Smith

HIGHWAY LOVE

Like lycanthropes call from the moon.
The highway is calling my name.
It feeds me deep down inside.
like the blood that flows through my veins.
The long winding road by my feet.
The Eagle that screams with each grip.
The wind pushed up on my brow
As the throttle is clutched for the trip.
Nothing left to hold on to.
Just the highway that's calling me out.
The life on the road is the purest.
It's the only true love I'm allowed.
By Mr. No One

CAN LOVE DERIVE FROM ADDICTION

Can love derive from addiction?

The blanket ideology of love,

Confusion without apology,

The catapult of hope,

Giving the suicidal nut a little more rope,

Commercialized into a fantasy,

Searching for the foundation of youth in misery,

Hegemony of deluded love,

Into a cheesy Hallmark card,

Became a common word without regard,

Lacking credibility and responsibility,

So finally, I gave up,

Not because of inequality,

It's the reality,

Reality of reincarnation,

The sameness radio station,

I don't want your parent's marriage,

Recreation of your old childhood scripts,

As you become your father,

And I your mother,

My dignity strips,

Violence, and screams elude me,

To owning my parent's marriage,

You are turning into my mother,

And I being my father,

This is not what I wanted,

Empty promises,

Bruises, and lies,

Punishment and award,

So, I abandon every plan we made,

Erase every promise I said,

No, love cannot derive from addiction.

By: Lucky Smith

SAMAELS VOW

In my plight of desperation.

Trying to hold on to what's been lost.

I lost myself.

I begged and pleaded.

I found myself crucified by my own wants and words.

I felt empty and hollow.

I felt physically ill at the ripping of my devotion.

The lack of emotion thrust in my direction.

It seemed as though all of my being

All of my giving's were a pointless misguided emptying of life.

All the blame is mine.

Now I see.

Now i know.

It took a task, but I've let go.

I've turned inside and saw what i kept away hidden for so long.

I am once again strong.

I hold no ill will.

However, all that was is now gone.

Thank you for the pain.

The dismissed coldness of gestures.

Thank you for the hurt that drove me insane.

It awoke the darkness within that needed to see life.

It was time.

For too long I crept in silence with Hope's not to return to who and what once I was.

It was displaced ideals.

A boy's dreams that are in reality nightmares.

It is foolish life for those who care.

Those who wish to share.

It is not for me.

Thank you for setting me free.

I am truly lost of you undoubtedly.

By Mr. No One

BORN TO LOVE YOU

I was born to love you

It was an appointment

I made without disappointment,

While this story ends with my heart broken,

It's a small token, you saved me

From tomorrow

From pity, regret and sorrow

Thank you for seeing in me

Something I didn't know

I could be

You believed in me

I still love you

It's the one thing

I know I can do

No matter how I use myself

No matter how much wealth

No matter how I abuse me

I can't erase what you see

No matter the facade of love affairs,

I smell you in the air

No matter the one-night stands

I am your biggest fan

No matter what I love you,

It's all I can do,

No matter how empty

I wake up in missing your memory

James not a day goes by

That I wished you didn't die

Death is not goodbye.

By: Lucky Smith

PENSIVE PARANOIA

We know it all till we don't know shit.

Till we're down on the floor taking the hit.

Took 45 and still alive.

Thought I had all the answers.

What a surprise.

I did this I did that.

I did more than I should.

I took to many chances and was up to no good.

Played several games.

Lost several times.

Sometimes I wish I could rewind.

But there's no going back.

No turning back the clock.

Sometimes we have very little time.

We've all been in a predicament that we thought we couldn't escape
I'm sure several can relate.

However, something or someone helped or intervened, and we
wondered what does it all mean.

As we grow things evolve.

We try to find a way to only have problems we can solve.

Some live in simplicity.

Some in chaos.

Some in between still trying to decide.

The red pill or the blue pill.

And some wishing they could just die or be killed.

Its prospective.

We need to be objective and sometimes.

We just need to listen and smell a rose.

Who knows?

No one ever truly has all the answers.

Life in itself is a question.

With the power of suggestion, we all know it all and dont know anything.

It's all a mood swing.

It's all a con.

From sunset till dawn.

All we do is try to figure it out.

Even when we don't think we have a plan.

We are trying to figure it out.

Trying to understand.

Till we wither away and realize.

Why didn’t I just embrace the day?

Why did I have to die?

By Mr. No One

DEAREST DADDY

Dearest Daddy,

I guess it's takes, getting shot to forgive you. I'm bleeding out and it takes the 911 dispatcher about 30 to 45 mins to get me help. My entire life is flashing before my eyes. I just want you to know, I love you. That doesn't change the past. Maybe, the love you gave was all you knew. Nonetheless, I'm dying. There's so much blood. I can't believe this is how I'm going to die. Honesty, daddy gunshot by a stalking ex-boyfriend. This is so cliche and boring, I'm pissed off. Why couldn't it be something just more interesting than this? I mean I have dated cool dudes than the stalker. Well, I guess how I die isn't that important. I have always flirted with the edge of death. Ironically, the moment I no longer want to flirt with danger, settle down and grow up. I fucking get shot in the stomach. WFT. Really, WFT. When I used and sold drugs nothing happens to me but getting caught by the police. When I lived my life as a teenage fuck up, never once got shot. Now that I am square. This moronic event happens. I wished I had more time. More time with my daughter, friends and family. More time to travel, and more time for hit up a few strip clubs. More time to earn my PHD. Just more time. I learn many lessons. Understood gray and lived passionately. I did go after all the goals I aspired for. Maybe, my life has been fully lived. Past occupations have included: drug dealer, retail, forestry fire fighter, bill collector, line server at a buffet, roofer, song writer, novelist, warehouse worker, model, food demo, night club promoter, actress, writer, poet, photographer, skip tracer, blogger, news reporter, editor, student and mother. I'm educated. This sucks, I'm dying now. But when is dying ever fun? I tried daddy to prevent from being murder by this stalker. I called the police, DA's office, told all my friends, hired an atty, domestic violence advocates and legal aid. I did everything I could to prevent this predictable incident. The judicial system just hasn't caught up with reality yet. When is life ever fair? When do insane individuals question their own rationale? It is what it is.

Love

Your Daughter

FORGET ME, FORGET YOU

As you leave my life,

I leave behind my pain.

As you turn to dust,

So does all my hurt.

As I leave you in my past,

I leave with you, my sorrow.

I burn you from my heart so it shall be,

Cast out of my memory.

Your memory erased from my mind,

No longer held by the constrains of time.

I accept this made manifest, so shall it be!"

An actual witch's spell to forget...

By Mr. No One

LOVERS AND TAXES

We live in a society filled with schizophrenic lovers. We crave love, need love, fear love and paranoid of attachment. We push and pull till there is nothing left. Drifters through life looking for anything. Schizophrenic lovers seeing something that never exist. Schizophrenic lovers missing reality. We make up this shrewd society. Baby bloomers babies, war propaganda aftermath. Raising children by neglect, and invisibility. It's no wonder the youth have so many sociopath-tic tendencies. The disconnections are so prevalent. Schizophrenic lovers' rule by bipolar laws. It's illegal to rob, unless there's tax identification to justify the brutality. It's illegal to kill, unless you are a cop. It's illegal to sell drugs, unless you are Johnson and Johnson. What's the point? Shape up, pay your bills, and dig into debt that you can never pay back. Consumerism has absolute control for the basic needs of life. Water, safety, clothes, food, shelter and love. Everything that is taxable is legal. For example, prostitution illegal, but porn is legal. Porn is a taxable item. Everything needed in order to survive comes with a price tag. Love itself is a concept that simply been complicated to the point that no one can understand it's true purpose, origin and benefits. The obfuscation is to mutilate the imagery of love; therefore, the complexity and falsehood can be put into a package with a shiny dangling sales tag attach. Just another faulty sales pitch. It's another lemon. Blame it on the devil in the mirror. Blame it on the man. Blame it on anything but me. Schizophrenic lovers, running without legs to walk.

By Lucky Smith

STUPID ME

Killed me from within.

How did I allow this?

Killed me from within.

How could I not see?

Killed me from within.

I said this couldn't happen.

Never not to me.

It's a cruel dark world we live in.

Can’t trust anyone.

Nothing said is truthful.

All trust is left undone.

Forget me

Forget you.

Forget a happy day.

From this point on I curse you.

You'll suffer my same way.

Inside you'll feel your crumbling.

Inside you’ll feel despair.

Inside your life I lost.

And you’ll feel like no one cares.

You should not have danced with the devil.

Because the devil will always lead.

I told you walk with caution.

But my words you didn’t heed.

Now you'll die like I did.

It's a killing from deep within.

You should have never looked my way.

You should have let me be.

I'm looking forward to your pain.

I'll watch you die from within.

No more time for talking.

It's time for your death to begin.

By Mr. No One

RAINBOW AFTER THE STORM

There is no recovery without honesty. Honesty, how I missed you. My addiction hid me from you. My addiction to affection, attention and ideology of love. The rabbit hole named addiction, finally appointed my deepest affliction. He was the ocean that drowned all my hopes and dreams. He was the perfect storm that rain manipulation, and confusion. He was the earthquake shaking my confidence and morals. He was the god of abuse, power and control. In his raging company, I couldn't see the exit sign. I lost my mind. Leaving everything I ever loved behind. We met during the road-trip with my addiction to love. I was so desperate for an instant guarantee. It was up to me to be free. It was my addiction feeding the dark void, that no one can avoid. I crawled away from the perfect storm, and I screamed no more. I ran to the arms of my whore. Soon after. I retired my favorite whore. No more, I whispered to my whore. No more empty sex. No more cleaning up another mess. My whore leaves the condom wrappers by the door, as he walks away. Crippled by silence on an empty bed I lay. Nothing satisfies this beast inside of me. Nothing fills this endless void. Throwing up pictures of the perfect storm into the air. The monster never cared. Photographs shatter on the bedroom floor. Captured lies on film. Captured hopes and dreams. For the first time I'm alone. No more, the perfect storm and the whore are gone. Another U-turn after another wrong turn. I blame myself for getting burn. So, honesty I come back to you. Cause without you I don't know what to do. I beg for your shelter. Without honesty nothing is ever what it seems. Without honesty realities are befuddled. I just got to take one more lightning strike, just one more time, to listen to his lies. One more day for this tragic story of his lies. Slowly the void begins to fill. The hole inside of me closes, as I let go of instant guarantees, ideologies of love and a thousand agreements. After the perfect storm passed over me for the last time, then came the rainbow. At the end of the rainbow is my dear friend. Friend, lover, and kind stranger. Tears in his eyes, he bandages my wounds from the war inside of me. He kisses my scars and holds me. He lets me walk, run and fall. He is a friend, and it is all I can ask for. I was lonely with my whore. Insanity invaded me with the perfect storm. So, my friend returns to me. And when I stop trying to control my destiny, honesty brought back sanity. Clarity of reality.

Honesty destroys the aftermath of the perfect storm. After the storm passed there is my friend, and my friend is my rainbow after the storm.

By: Lucky Smith

NOT AGAIN

I’m never gonna fall for you.

I’ll never make your dreams come true.

I’m not the magic man you seek.

I’ll never make your knees go weak.

I’ve tried before.

it didn't work. it ended bad.

I became a jerk.

I’d rather not be that way again.

So before I start ill just make it end.

I’m never gonna want to try.

I’m not gonna let you make me cry.

I’ll control the fears and keep it true.

I’m never gonna fall for you.

By Mr NoOne

WRAPPED UP

I wrapped up all my hopes and dreams,

Laugher turned into screams,

How did this happen?

Why did this happen?

Two fucked up people together

Couldn't scale the stormy weather

We seek recovery

the logic is flawed I see

No matter what

Therapy or couple's therapy

Can't stop what can never be,

Our brokenness made sense to me

I gave all I had

So much I'm mad

Obsess with what we could be

Destroyed by what we will never see

Floating on the sea of shame

I am a shell that's cracking and breaking

All I wanted was for him to love me

But

The lies physically set me free

Entrapment by promises

My poetry drives him to drink

I'm sick I can't think

Is he safe?

I scream at myself

Don't fucking care

His love never was there

Is he okay?

How did we end up this way?

I am haunted by the past

My feelings shatter my mask

All I wanted was a healthy relationship

with my perfect storm

No one else fills this void

His memory I can't avoid.

By Lucky Smith

NARCISSIST

Why would I care if they don’t?

Why should I care if they won’t?

Why should I give

This part of me when

Giving is all that I do.

They don’t care about me.

I finally see.

And I'm finally saying FUCK YOU!

People will say they love you.

People will say they care.

People will say they think of you.

With never a minute to spare.

They find some time for others yet for you never a minute or two.

They say words they don’t know like I love you.

And now the words that I use are FUCK YOU!

Take all your bullshit and promises.

Take all the lies that you spew.

Everyone gets what's deserving.

One day you'll get what is due.

I thought maybe this was different.

But to me your just like the rest.

Never again will this happen.

I'll never again give my best.

So go on and do what you're going to.

I'm taking this in as is true.

But one day you'll see what is inside of me and all I will say is FUCK YOU!!

By Mr. No One

THE CYCLE

I scream at him,

Just go away, leave me alone,

I'm not home,

My bones are pushing him away,

Being alone is just easier anyway,

Alone in my room,

In front of the screen,

I'm craving it,

Anything just be alone,

Being alone to drown in my porn,

Alone to obsess over making myself to feel,

Alone to find away not to feel,

So, I'm craving it again,

Anything but recovery,

Then what's next?

Weeks, months of indulging in my addiction to porn,

To the fantasy that desensitizes me,

Then the realization of being alone sets in,

So, I go online, this battle I can't win,

Next person to date, try to love,

Then what?

I feel trap, suffocated, I want out,

So, the cycle repeats again and again,

By Lucky Smith

DERAILED

I see my way out.

I see it each day.

Life’s annihilation.

In my head like a movie, it plays.

I see all that's happened

I see my demise.

At the end of the tunnel.

Will I find a prize?

Shadows of sins I've committed

Stay by my side.

From myself I can’t run.

From myself I can’t hide.

I see only loss.

I see nothing else.

I'm searching in darkness.

To make this come true.

One minute more and all pain will be through

By Mr. No One

OLD LOVE MAPS

What was your most traumatic experience besides what's going on now? -Ask the doctor

How can the only man that was healthy enough to love me without abuse cause me so much despair? Sometimes the predictable is safer than healthy and normal. James was safe, balance, normal, stable, and healthy. Predictions gives moments in illusion of control. He was the first man I was attracted to that share no emotional attributes of my father. James was nerd but in a hot way. He never used drugs or any type of addict. We were proof opposites attract. He still is the man I want to marry, but that can't happen. I was in shock how I adored him. His brilliance sent me to ecstasy. He was emotionally available, educated, kind, generous, romantic and sexy. Yet, I ran from him but only to run back to him. James never hurt me intentionally in anyway. But he is the one man that damaged me just as any of my past abusers. He never cheated or lie. My thoughts, needs and wants always mattered to him. He buried my old love maps from my childhood. Without trying he created new love maps. He wrote the directions so directly and eloquently, that my reality became a fairytale. Then doctors make mistakes, life fucking happens and none of it is ever fair. Coming home and finding my fiancé dead. Not a day goes by without me missing him, wishing he was alive, I wished I cherish every moment with him. But we take the ordinary days for granted. but when you're young you assume for more tomorrows to come. So, my most hideous moment was December 20. He was the only person who was my best friend, he was my partner. Losing him was the most fucking tragic moment of my life. Years later all the love maps James buried resurfaced. So that's why my life has so many emotional vampires, abusers, different variations of my father and chaos now. The old love maps came back. Now it's time to burn the old love maps.

By Lucky Smith

CARNIVORE

Devastation of the soul

The mind to follow.

In a well of self-loathing.

Sadness of what's transpired.

Something taken none can return

Inside I burn.

Inside I yearn to be complete.

Never to look back at that day's defeat.

Unable to fight.

No one hears my screams for help.

This is hell.

All I can do is allow the destruction of this shell.

Take what you will.

Inside I'm now dead.

I'm lost in my own head.

Reliving this over and over.

Will it ever end?

By Mr. No One

I FUCKING HATE YOU

Hurry up and talk more shit,

I won't scream and hit back...

I'm smiling cause you on camera,

I hate to hate you,

Since I know you most of life,

Thank you I was never your wife,

Hang me out to dry,

And watch me fly,

Print this one for the judge too,

I FUCKING HATE YOU!!!

Explain to me how I was hot when I was 12 years old,

You are a pedophile fucking sicko,

You were a man, and I was a child,

I stay for awhile,

Under your sick fantasies,

You are so sick and dirty,

First you exploited me,

Then I blame myself,

Fuck with mind and health,

Introduce me to drugs,

So, I was easy to control,

You are a sick ass hoe,

I have spent over $10,000 dollars in therapy,

Cause I had your fucking baby,

You are a dirty piece of shit,

So go on swing take another hit,

For the last 15 years has been like swallowing glass,

So, kiss my ass,

I AM TELLING THE JUDGE GOD DAMN THING!!!

You are still hanging out hunting for your next victim

You are a fucking pig,

One last thing I FUCKING HATE YOU!

By: Lucky Smith

TAKE THIS ALL

Take this all away.

I don’t wanna feel today.

Take this all away.

Save it for another day just take this all away.

I don’t want to feel no more.

Take this all just take this all away.

Every day I'm looking at the mirror and I see

Everything that falls apart

Is right in front of me.

Nothing seems to stay the same it all just meets its end.

I don’t want to do this no more I don’t want to pretend.

So, take it all away

Take this all away.

I don’t wanna feel today.

Take this all away.

Save it for another day just take this all away.

I don’t want to feel no more.

Take this all just take this all away

I see you staring back at me and I don’t know what to say.

Why can’t this all just be a different and better day.

It should have been more than this.

What' is wrong with me.

Sometimes I don’t want to be.

But you can’t

I can’t.

Take this all away

Take this all away.

I don’t wanna feel today.

Take this all away.

Save it for another day just take this all away.

I don’t want to feel no more.

Take this all just take this all away

Can’t save myself

I can’t save you.

I can’t help anyone.

What in this life have I done?

But I can’t stop

And I can’t run.

If I could I'd leave it all

And never look again.

But I'll be here until my end.

Or until someone takes it all away.

Take this all away.

I don’t wanna feel today.

Take this all away.

Save it for another day just take this all away.

I don’t want to feel no more.

Take this all just take this all away

Please I don’t want to stay.

So, take it all take it all

You can have it all just take it all away.

By Mr. No One

www.ingramcontent.com/pod-product-compliance
Lightning Source LLC
LaVergne TN
LVHW050011170826
845677LV00023B/3617

* 9 7 9 8 8 3 1 6 0 2 3 5 7 *